A Biography
of Malcolm X

by Jessica Gunderson
illustrated by Seitu Hayden

Consultant:
Keith Mayes, PhD
Professor of History and
African American and African Studies
University of Minnesota, Minneapolis

CAPSTONE PRESS
a capstone imprint

X

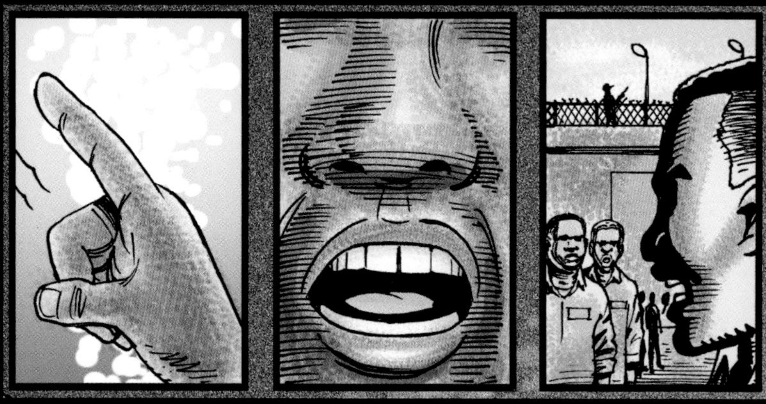

Graphic Library is published by Capstone Press,
151 Good Counsel Drive, P.O. Box 669,
Mankato, Minnesota 56002.

www.capstonepub.com

Library of Congress Cataloging-in-Publication Data
Gunderson, Jessica.
X : the biography of Malcolm X / by Jessica Gunderson ; illustrated by Seitu Hayden.
p. cm.—(Graphic Library. American graphic)
Summary: "In graphic novel format, explores the life and death of Malcolm X"—Provided by publisher.
Includes bibliographical references and index.
ISBN 978-1-4296-5471-5 (library binding)
ISBN 978-1-4296-6267-3 (paperback)
1. X, Malcolm, 1925-1965—Juvenile literature. 2. African American Muslims—Biography—Juvenile literature. I. Hayden, Seitu. II. Title.
BP223.Z8G86 2011
297.8'7092—dc22
[B] 2010037029

Printed in the United States of America in Stevens Point, Wisconsin.
092010 005934WZS11

Direct quotations appear in yellow on the following pages:

Pages 12-13, 22 (second and third panels), and 29, from *By Any Means Necessary: Speeches, Interviews, and a Letter by Malcolm X,* George Breitman, ed. (New York: Pathfinder Press, 1970)

Page 17, from *Malcolm X Speaks: Selected Speeches and Statements,* George Breitman, ed. (New York: Merit Publishers, 1965)

Pages 20, 21, 24, and 27, from The *Autobiography of Malcolm X* by Malcolm X and Alex Haley (New York: Grove Press, 1966)

Page 22 (first panel), from *The Last Year of Malcolm X: The Evolution of a Revolutionary,* George Breitman, ed. (New York: Merit Publishers, 1967)

Art Director: Nathan Gassman

Editor: Lori Shores

Media Researcher: Wanda Winch

Production Specialist: Eric Manske

Photo Credits:
Library of Congress, Prints and Photographs Division, 28

6

During this time, black people could not use the same bathrooms or water fountains as whites. They had to sit at the back of buses and go to separate schools. Some people believed blacks and whites should be treated equally. But Elijah believed that black people should form their own society. Malcolm spoke about Elijah's ideas to fellow prisoners.

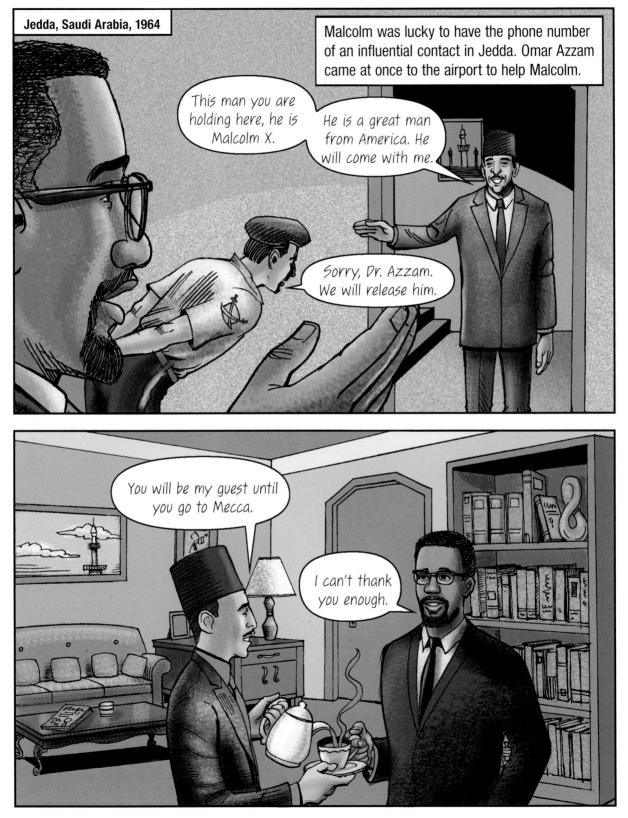

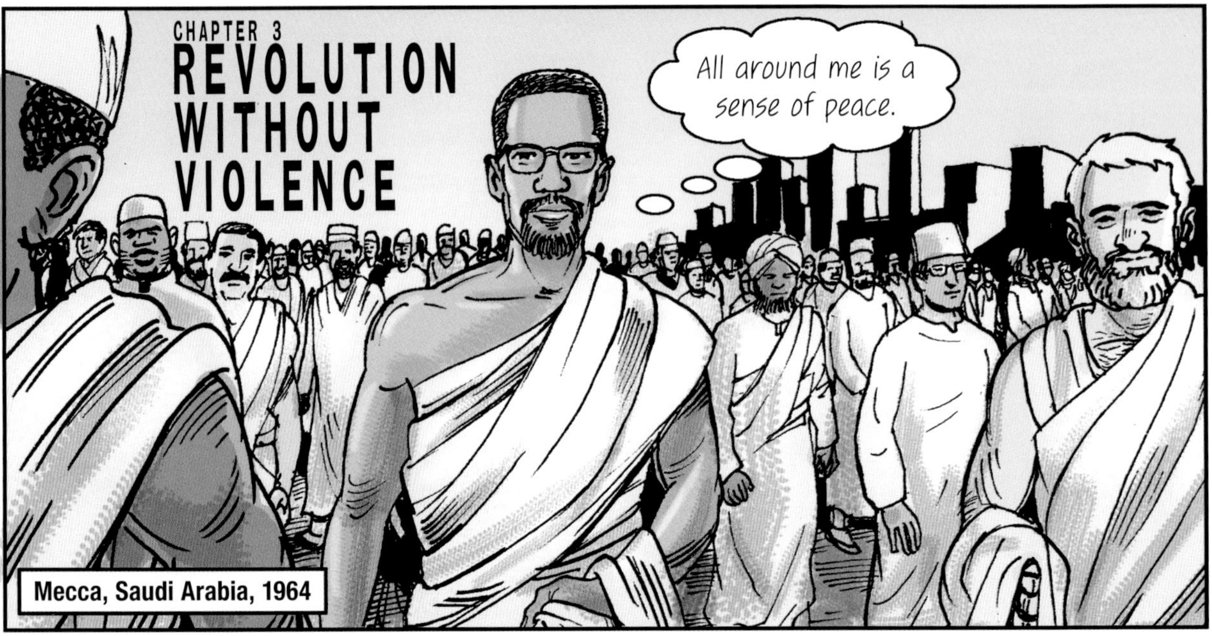
CHAPTER 3
REVOLUTION WITHOUT VIOLENCE
All around me is a sense of peace.
Mecca, Saudi Arabia, 1964

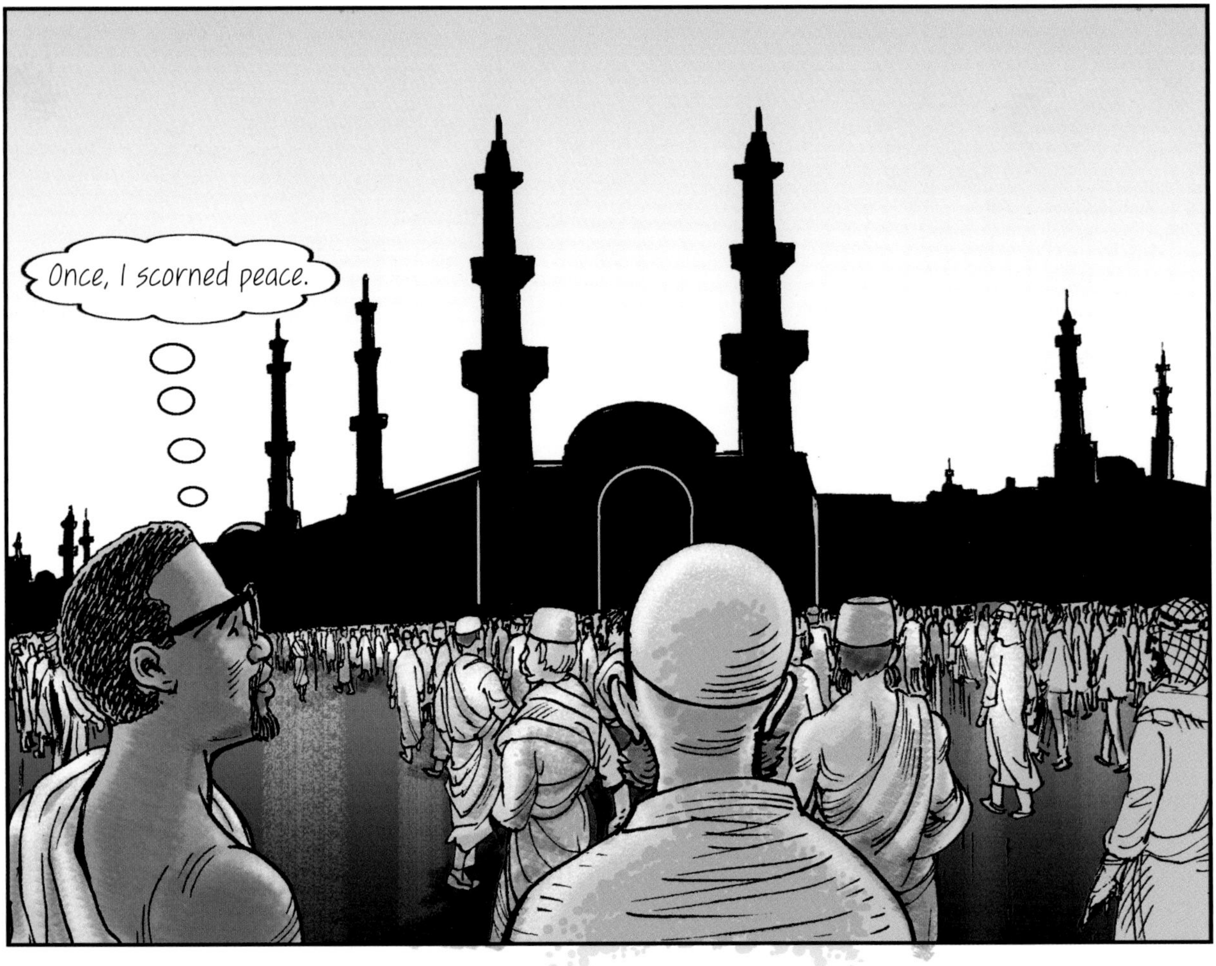
Once, I scorned peace.

17

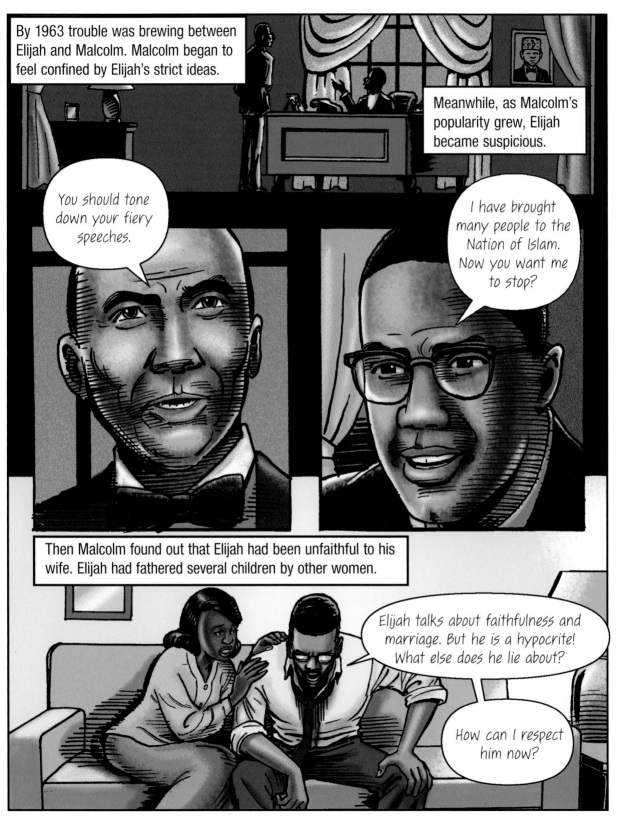

By 1963 trouble was brewing between Elijah and Malcolm. Malcolm began to feel confined by Elijah's strict ideas.

Meanwhile, as Malcolm's popularity grew, Elijah became suspicious.

You should tone down your fiery speeches.

I have brought many people to the Nation of Islam. Now you want me to stop?

Then Malcolm found out that Elijah had been unfaithful to his wife. Elijah had fathered several children by other women.

Elijah talks about faithfulness and marriage. But he is a hypocrite! What else does he lie about?

How can I respect him now?

December 1, 1963

The split between Malcolm and Elijah soon grew even wider. When President John F. Kennedy was assassinated, Elijah warned Malcolm not to speak about it.

Kennedy's assassination shows the hatred typical of whites. It's a case of chickens coming home to roost.

Many people thought Malcolm was saying that Kennedy deserved to die. Later Malcolm explained that he meant violence leads to more violence. But his explanation came too late for Elijah.

You have disobeyed my orders!

You are suspended from the Nation of Islam for 90 days.

You're suspending me after all my hard work?

Malcolm never returned to the Nation of Islam.

Instead he formed his own group, Muslim Mosque, and later, the Organization of Afro-American Unity.

I wish that Americans could learn to live as one ...

... rather than always fighting against each other.

Malcolm wrote letters to his family and friends telling about his experiences at Mecca. He also wrote to Muslim Mosque, asking that the letter be published.

Americans will be shocked. To them, hatred and I go hand-in-hand.

MORE ABOUT MALCOLM X

Although labeled by the public as a militant black man, Malcolm X had a likeable personality and charm. He often wore a smile and liked to make people laugh. He spoke in a way that young and old, educated and uneducated would understand.

Malcolm had a difficult childhood. When he was just six years old, his father was hit by a streetcar and killed. Some people believed he had been beaten and pushed onto the tracks by white racists. When he was 13 years old, Malcolm's mother was sent to a mental hospital. Malcolm and his 10 siblings were sent to separate foster homes. He dropped out of school after the eighth grade and soon became involved in criminal activities.

After prison Malcolm continued to read books on history, religion, and philosophy. He slept only four hours each night. He hoped that the black community would follow his example and become as educated as possible. He said, "Education is the passport to the future, for tomorrow belongs to those who prepare for it today."

Malcolm's wife and other members of his family continued to spread Malcolm's ideas after his death. The civil rights movement continued throughout the 1960s and helped gain equality for African Americans in the workplace and society. The struggle against racism, however, continues to this day.

Malcolm X expressed the struggles and attitudes of the African American in a way that hadn't been voiced before. He died before being able to fully explore his newfound ideas on race, equality, and unity. Nonetheless, Malcolm X played an important role in the struggle for human rights and left behind a lasting legacy.

I BELIEVE IN HUMAN BEINGS, AND THAT ALL HUMAN BEINGS SHOULD BE RESPECTED AS SUCH, REGARDLESS OF THEIR COLOR.

—MALCOLM X

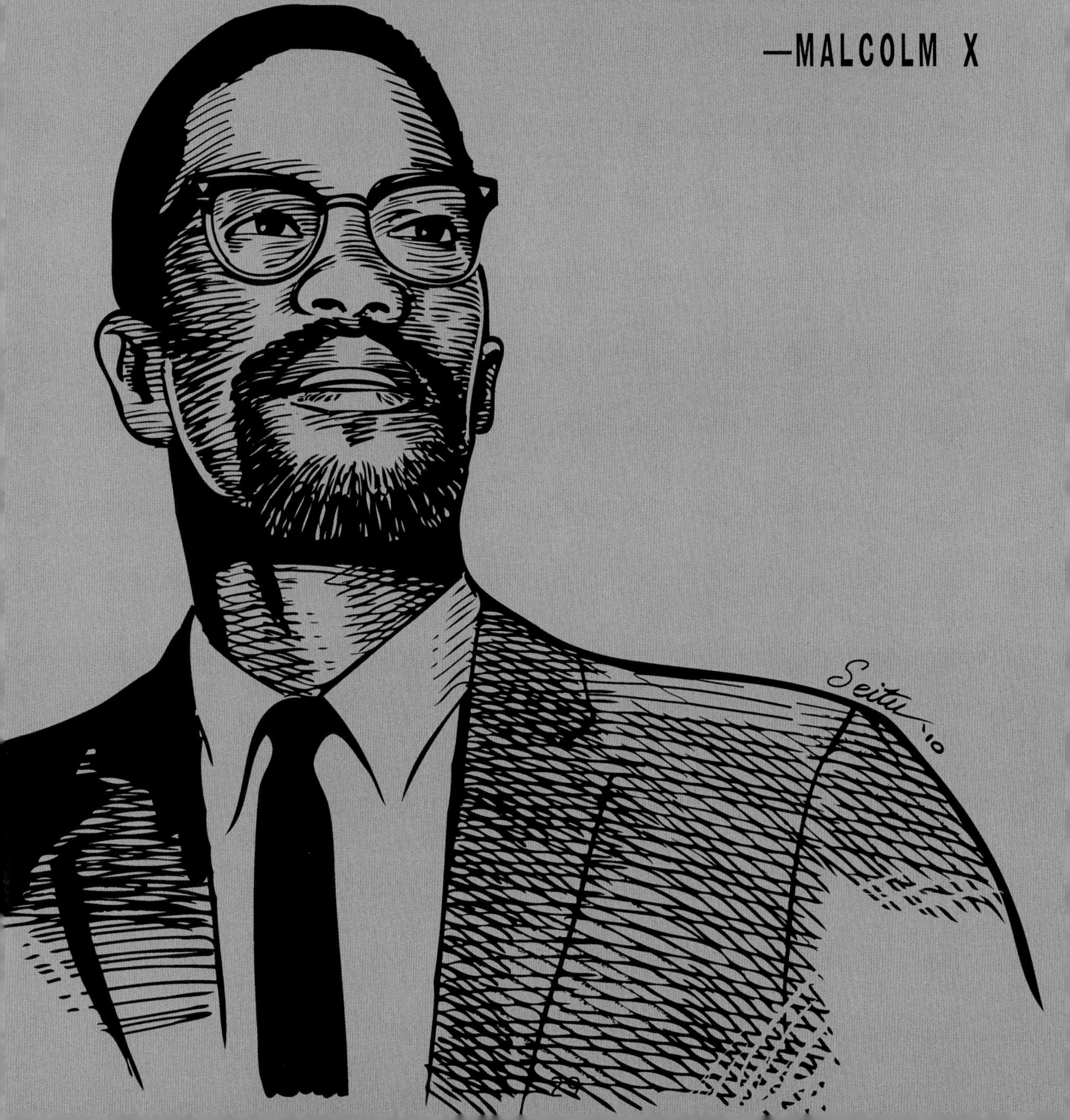
Seitz '10

GLOSSARY

articulate (ar-TIK-yuh-luht)—able to express oneself clearly in words

assassinate (uh-sa-suh-NAYT)—to murder a well-known or important person, such as a president

compromise (KAHM-pruh-myz)—an agreement that people with different views reach after each gives up some demands

equality (i-KWAH-luh-tee)—the same rights for everyone

hostile (HOSS-tuhl)—unfriendly or angry

hypocrite (HIP-uh-krit)—someone who pretends to be loyal, honest, or good

ignorant (IG-nur-uhnt)—not educated, or not knowing about many things

imprison (im-PRIZ-uhn)—to put someone in prison, or to lock the person up

influential (in-floo-EN-shuhl)—having the power to change or affect someone or something

justice (JUHSS-tiss)—fair behavior or treatment

militant (MIL-uh-tuhnt)—prepared to fight or be very aggressive in support of a cause

mourn (MORN)—to be very sad and miss someone who has died

passionate (PASH-uh-nit)—having or showing very strong feelings

pilgrimage (PIL-gruhm-uhj)—a trip to an important religious place

revolution (rev-uh-LOO-shun)—a rebellion by a group of people against a system of government or a way of life

scorn (SKORN)—to treat with a feeling of hatred or disrespect

segregation (seg-ruh-GAY-shuhn)—the practice of keeping groups of people apart, especially based on race

spokesperson (SPOKES-pur-suhn)—someone who is chosen to speak publicly for a group

READ MORE

Banting, Erinn. *The Civil Rights Movement.* African
American History. New York: Weigl Publishers, 2009.

Gormley, Beatrice. *Malcolm X: A Revolutionary Voice.*
Sterling Biographies. New York: Sterling Publishing,
2008.

Mis, Melody S. *Meet Malcolm X.* Civil Rights Leaders.
New York: PowerKids Press, 2008.

INTERNET SITES

FactHound offers a safe, fun way to find Internet sites related to
this book. All of the sites on FactHound have been researched by
our staff.

Here's all you do: Visit *www.facthound.com*

Type in this code: 9781429654715

Super-cool stuff!

Check out projects, games and lots more at
www.capstonekids.com

INDEX